# FIRST SCIENCE LIBRARY
# Up in the Air

- 17 EASY-TO-FOLLOW EXPERIMENTS FOR LEARNING FUN
- FIND OUT ABOUT FLIGHT AND HOW WEATHER WORKS!

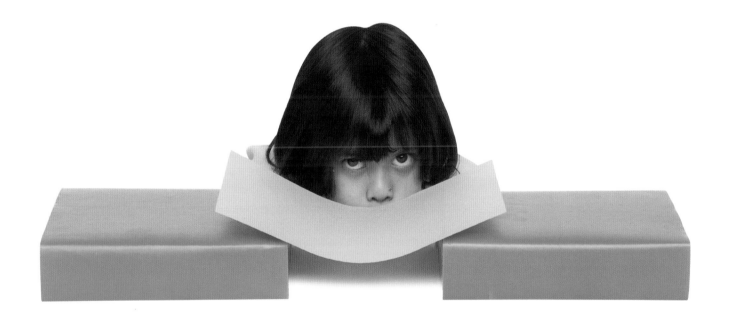

WENDY MADGWICK

ARMADILLO

This edition is published by Armadillo, an imprint of Anness Publishing Ltd, 108 Great Russell Street, London WC1B 3NA; info@anness.com

www.annesspublishing.com

If you like the images in this book and would like to investigate using them for publishing, promotions or advertising, then please visit our website www.practicalpictures.com for more information.

Publisher: Joanna Lorenz
Designer: Anita Ruddell
Photographer: Andrew Sydenham

Many thanks to Aneesah, Ben, Jasmine, John, May and Poppy for appearing in the book
Illustrations: Catherine Ward/ Simon Girling Associates
Production Controller: Wendy Lawson

PUBLISHER'S NOTE
Although the advice and information in this book are believed to be accurate and true at the time of going to press, neither the authors nor the publisher can accept any legal responsibility or liability for any errors or omissions that may have been made nor for any inaccuracies nor for any loss, harm or injury that comes about from following instructions or advice in this book.

Words that appear in **bold** in the text are explained in the glossary on page 32.

Manufacturer: Anness Publishing Ltd,
108 Great Russell Street,
London WC1B 3NA, England
For Product Tracking go to:
www.annesspublishing.com/tracking
Batch: 7006-22864-1127

# Contents

# Looking at air

This book has lots of fun activities to help you find out about air. Here are some simple rules you should follow before doing an activity.

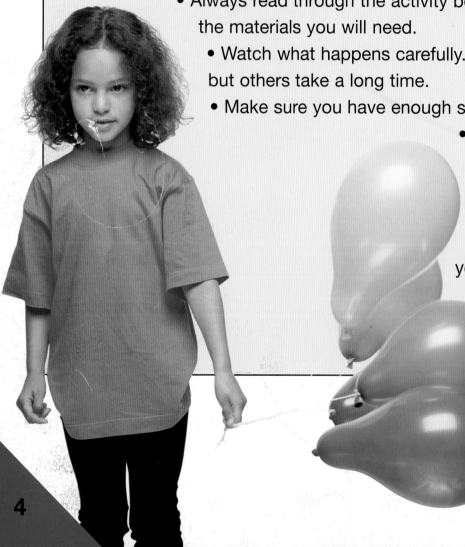

- Always tell a grown-up what you are doing. Ask him or her if you may do the activity.
- Always read through the activity before you begin. Collect all the materials you will need.
- Watch what happens carefully. Some things happen quickly, but others take a long time.
- Make sure you have enough space to set up your activity.
- Follow the steps carefully. Ask a grown-up to help you cut things.
- Keep a notebook. Draw pictures or write down what you did and what happened.
- Always clear up when you have finished. Wash your hands.

▶ The air inside this balloon is heated by burners. Hot air rises and lifts the balloon into the air.

4

# Air? Where?

Air is all around us. But we cannot see it. We cannot taste it or touch it. So how do we know it is there? Let's find out.

**Blow it out**
Put your hand up in front of your mouth. Now pucker up your lips and blow. What can you feel? You can feel the air blowing on your hand, but you cannot see it.

## Fan it

**You will need:**
sheet of paper,
sticky tape
or stapler.

**1** Take a sheet of paper. Fold over one side. Turn the paper over. Fold again.

**2** Keep on turning and folding the paper. Tape or staple one end.

**3** Wave your fan in front of your face. Can you feel the air moving?

## Bubbles

**You will need:** empty bottle, bowl, water.

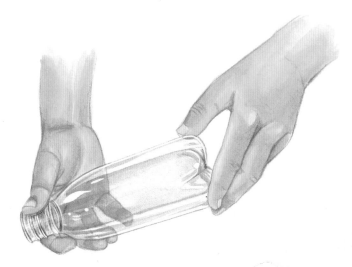

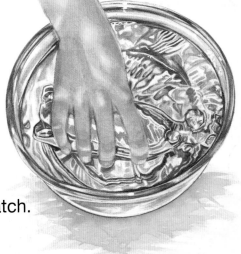

**2** Fill a bowl with water. Push the bottle under the water. Watch.

**1** Take the empty bottle. What is in it?

Can you see bubbles coming out? They are bubbles of air. The water going into the bottle forced the air out. So air takes up space and is all around you.

7

# Weigh it up

Air is all around us. It takes up space. But does it weigh anything? How can we find out?

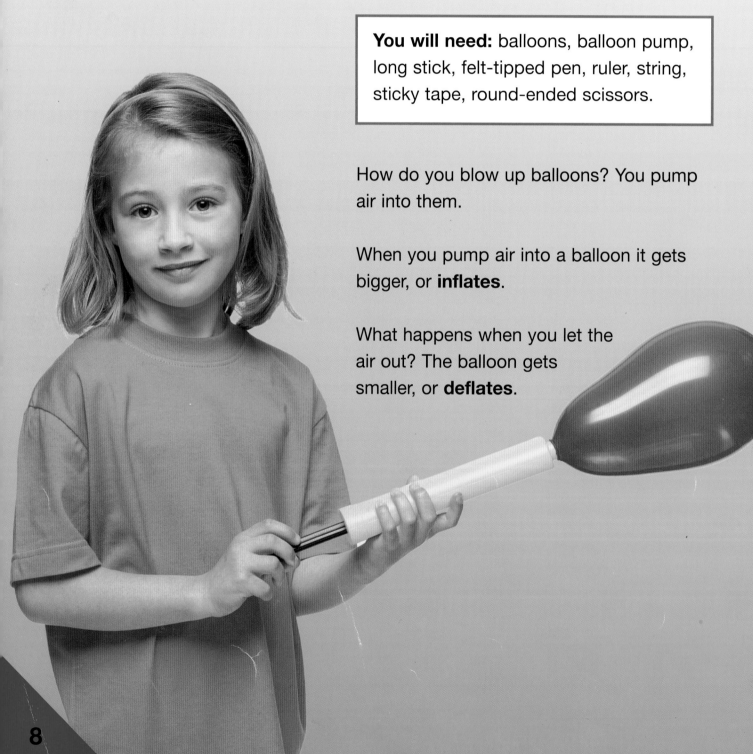

**You will need:** balloons, balloon pump, long stick, felt-tipped pen, ruler, string, sticky tape, round-ended scissors.

How do you blow up balloons? You pump air into them.

When you pump air into a balloon it gets bigger, or **inflates**.

What happens when you let the air out? The balloon gets smaller, or **deflates**.

# Light as air

We can weigh air using two balloons.

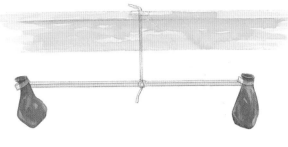

**1** Mark the middle of a long stick.

**3** Cut two pieces of sticky tape the same size. Tape one balloon to each end of the stick. Make sure the stick is still level.

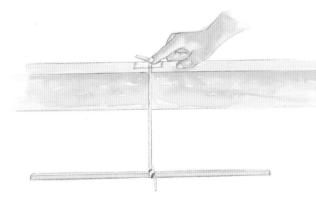

**2** Tie a piece of string round the middle of the stick. Tape the other end to the edge of a table. Make sure the stick is level.

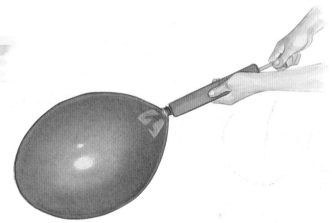

**4** Unstick one balloon and blow it up. Ask a grown-up to tie it.

**5** Retape the balloon to the same place on the stick. Does the stick stay level? Which end goes down?

The end with the blown-up balloon will go down. It is heavier than the empty balloon. Air has weight.

# Air power

Like all objects, air is pulled down to the ground by **gravity**. As air is pulled down it presses on things. This is called **air pressure**.

> **You will need:** ruler, large sheet of paper, two drinking glasses, clear film (plastic wrap), sticky tape, a straw, box, round-ended scissors, washable felt-tipped pen, thin cardboard.

Put a ruler on the table. Make sure part of it lies over the edge. Put a sheet of paper on top of the ruler. Gently hit the end of the ruler.

Does the paper lift up? Can you feel something pressing down on the paper?

Air presses down on the paper.

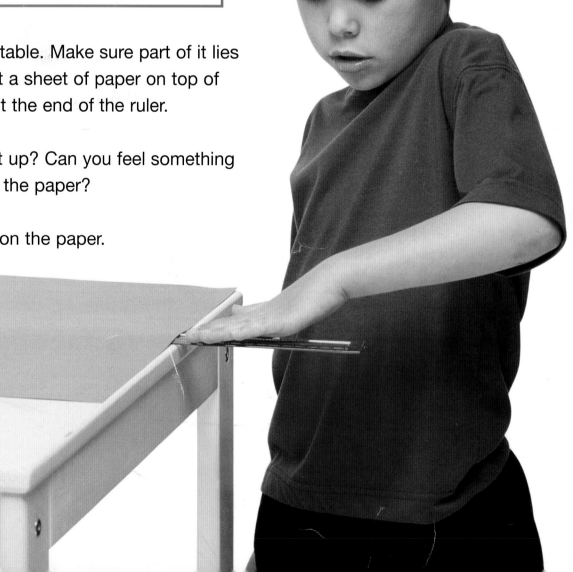

# High or low?

Air pressure can tell us about the **weather**. High pressure means good weather. Low pressure means bad weather.

**1** Cover a glass with clear film. Tape the film in place.

**2** Cut one end of a straw into a point. Mark the pointer in black. Tape the other end to the middle of the clear film.

**3** Take another glass. Put the glasses next to each other in a shoe box. Make a cardboard rule with narrow divisions as shown. Tape it to the other glass so that the pointer points to 0. Keep the box away from windows, doors and breezes.

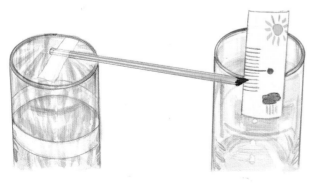

**4** Look at the pointer each day. If it moves down, the air pressure is lower.

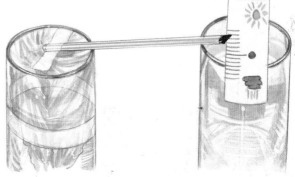

**5** If the pointer moves up, the air pressure is higher.

11

# Up, up and away

Warm air takes up more space than cold air. It is also lighter. This means warm air rises.

## Blow up

Can warm air blow up a balloon on its own? Try it and see.

**You will need:** balloon, plastic bottle, large bowl, warm water, ice.

**1** Stretch a balloon over the end of a plastic bottle.

**2** Hold the bottle in a bowl of warm water. What happens?

The air inside the bottle gets warmer and **expands** so the balloon inflates.

**3** Add lots of ice to the water. What happens?

The air in the bottle gets colder and **contracts** so the balloon deflates. Warm air takes up more room than cold air.

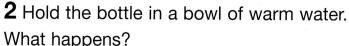

# Spinning snakes!

Does hot air rise? Find out using a snake mobile.

**You will need:** cotton thread, a straw, pencils or washable felt-tipped pens in various shades, round-ended scissors, sticky tape. You will need to hang something over a warm radiator.

**1** Tie cotton thread around the middle of a straw.

**2** Draw two snake shapes on a piece of paper, and cut out the shapes.

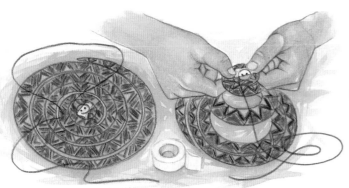

**3** Tape thread to the top of each snake.

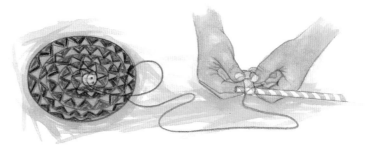

**4** Tape the snakes to either end of the straw.

**5** Hang the mobile over a warm radiator, making sure the straw is level. Make another mobile. Hang it in the middle of the room. Which snakes move the most?

Warm air rises. This moving air makes the snakes hanging above the warm radiator spin faster.

13

# Keep warm

A warm object cools down if it is in a cold place. Heat from the warm object goes into the cold air. Air can help to keep things warm.

Penguin chicks are covered in thick ▶ fur, which helps them to keep warm. Air is caught among the fur.

## Cover up

**You will need:** five jars of the same size, wool scarf, box, scrap paper or newspapers, sheet of thick paper, sticky tape, round-ended scissors, thick plastic, very warm (but not boiling) water.

**1** Collect five jars of the same size. Wrap a wool scarf loosely around jar 1.

**2** Fill a box and lid with crumpled paper. Put jar 2 in the middle.

**3** Wrap thick paper around jar 3. Pull it tight. Tape it in place. Cover the lid with paper.

**4** Wrap jar 4 in thick plastic. Pull it tight. Tape in place. Cover the lid with plastic. Leave jar 5 without any wrapping.

**5** Pour very warm (not boiling) water into each jar. Put on the lids and covers. Cover the lid of jar 1 with the scarf. Put the lid on the box of jar 2. Leave the jars for about an hour.

**6** Take off the lid of each jar. Test the water with your finger. The water in jars 1 and 2 should be warmest. The air trapped in the wrappings helped to keep the water warm. We call this **insulation**.

# On the move

Moving air does not press on objects as much as still air. It does not have as much pushing power.

## Dip it!

Try to blow a piece of paper away.

**You will need:** two large books of same thickness, large sheet of paper.

**1** Put the books on a table.

**2** Place a piece of paper over the books.

**3** Blow underneath the paper. What happens to the paper? The paper dips down as you blow. The still air above the paper pushes it down.

# Swing it

Can you blow two plastic bricks apart?

**You will need:** string, two small plastic bricks, sticky tape, round-ended scissors.

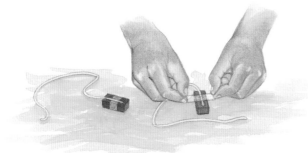

**1** Tape string to two of the bricks.

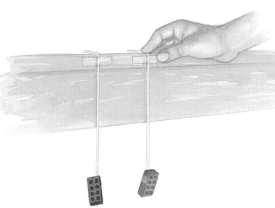

**2** Tape the strings to the edge of a table. They should be about 6cm/2in apart. Make sure the bricks can swing freely. Hold them still.

**3** Let go of the bricks. Blow hard in between the bricks.

What happens to the bricks? The bricks don't swing apart, they swing together!

A **cyclone** is a mass of air that swirls around and around. It can cause a lot of damage to property. This one is approaching Florida, USA.

# Up we go

Moving air has less pushing power than still air. Flying animals and aircraft use moving air to keep up in the air. They all have specially shaped wings.

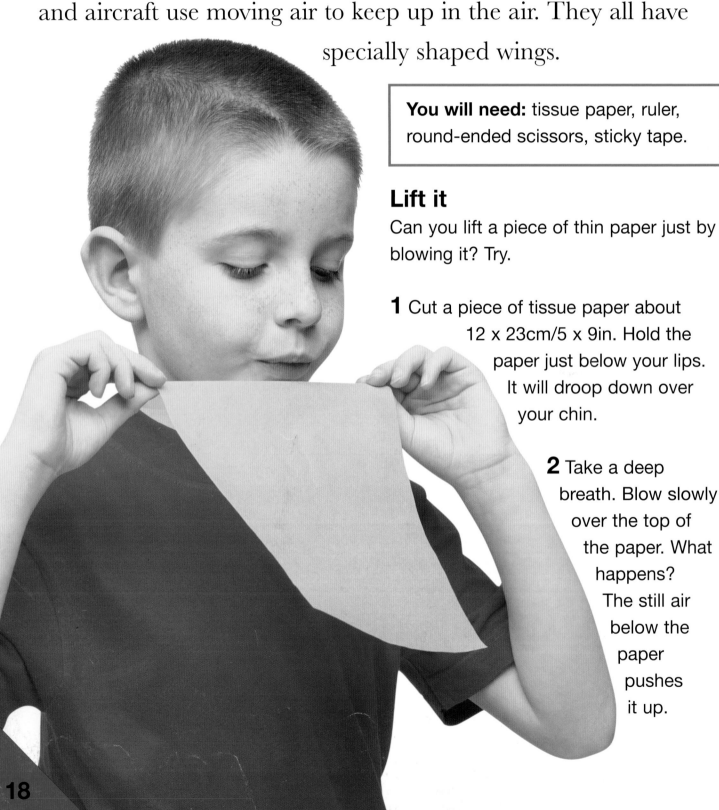

> **You will need:** tissue paper, ruler, round-ended scissors, sticky tape.

## Lift it

Can you lift a piece of thin paper just by blowing it? Try.

**1** Cut a piece of tissue paper about 12 x 23cm/5 x 9in. Hold the paper just below your lips. It will droop down over your chin.

**2** Take a deep breath. Blow slowly over the top of the paper. What happens? The still air below the paper pushes it up.

# Wing power

Does the shape of a wing help it rise? Let's see.

**1** Cut two pieces of tissue paper about 22 x 10cm/9 x 4in. Fold them in half with a sharp crease.

**2** Tape the edges of one piece of tissue paper together.

**3** Take the other piece of paper. Put the top half about 2cm/1in from the edge of the bottom. Tape in place.

**4** Slide a ruler into the straight wing. Hold the ruler about 5cm/2in in front of your mouth. Take a deep breath. Blow slowly. What happens to the paper wing? It does not rise into the air.

**5** Try again with the curved wing. What happens? The curved paper wing rises into the air as you blow.

# Let's fly

Flying animals and aircraft have a smooth shape. This helps them fly well. We say they are **streamlined**.

Look at these pictures. The bird and plane have a smooth shape. Do you think this helps them fly? Try this next test and see.

## Dart about

**You will need:** three sheets of A4 or letter paper, round-ended scissors, sticky tape.

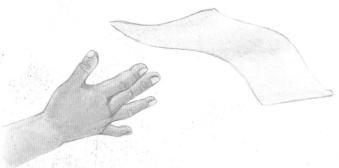

**1** Throw one sheet of paper into the air. How well does it fly?

**2** Now screw up the paper into a ball. Throw it. How well does it fly?

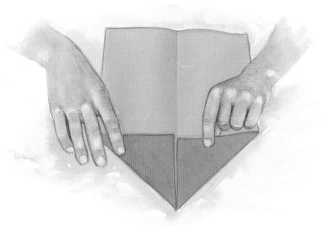

**3** Now make a streamlined dart. Fold a piece of paper down the middle. Open the paper. Fold over the top corners. Make sure they meet in the middle.

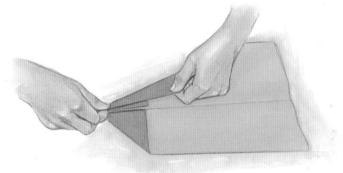

**4** Fold the corners into the middle as shown.

**5** Now fold the sides into the middle. Cut off the ends.

**6** Turn the dart over. Fold the sides together. Pull out the sides to make the wings. Tape the top of the wings together.

Now try to fly it. How well does it fly? Does it fly better than the flat piece of paper? Does it go further than the paper ball? Does the dart have a smooth shape? Is this why it flies so well?

# Model plane

The scientific rules of flying are the same for any aircraft, from a huge airliner to this model made out of paper and a drinking straw. Making this model allows you to see how control surfaces, such as the aileron, rudder and elevators, work.

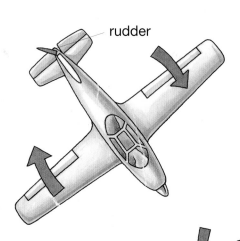

rudder

To turn the aircraft (yaw), the pilot turns the rudder to one side.

To make the aircraft descend or climb (pitch), the pilot adjusts the elevators on the tailplane.

elevator

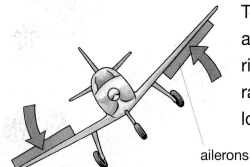

To roll (tilt or bank) the aircraft to the left or right, the ailerons are raised on one wing and lowered on the other.

ailerons

## Glide along
**You will need:** pencil, set square, ruler, paper, scissors, glue stick, sticky tape, drinking straw.

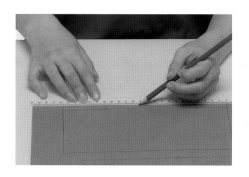

**1** Draw two rectangles, 22 x 10cm/8¾ x 4in and 20 x 3.5cm/8 x 1¼in. Mark ailerons 6 x 1cm/2½ x ½in on two corners of the larger one. Cut out two elevators 3.5 x 1cm/ 1½ x ½in on the other.

**2** Make the wings. Wrap the larger rectangle over a pencil and glue along the edges. Remove the pencil and make cuts along the 1cm/½in lines to allow the ailerons to move.

**3** Make the tail. Fold the smaller rectangle into a W shape. Glue its middle to make the fin. Cut along the two 1cm/½in lines. Make a 1cm/½in cut on the fin to make a rudder.

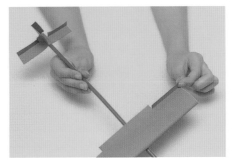

**6** Bend the left-hand aileron up and the right-hand aileron down the same amount. Bend the rudder to the left. This will make the plane turn to the left as it flies.

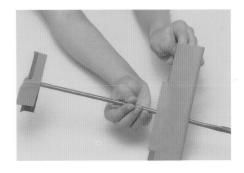

**7** Bend the right-hand aileron up and the left-hand aileron down. Bend the rudder to the right slightly and the plane will turn to the right. Can you make it fly in a circle?

**4** Tape the wings and tail to the drinking straw (the plane's body). Position the wings about one quarter of the way along the straw.

Launch your plane by throwing it steadily straight ahead. To make it fly even farther, you could use paper clips or non-hardening clay to weight the nose.

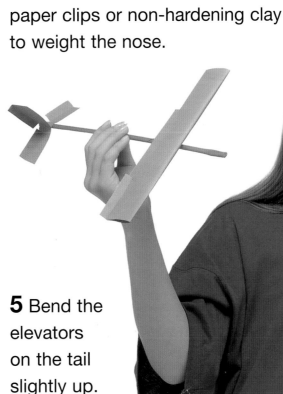

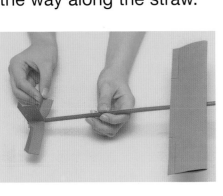

**5** Bend the elevators on the tail slightly up. This will make the plane climb as it flies. Bend the elevators down to make it dive.

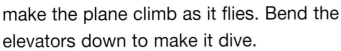

# Air lift

When you pump up a tyre, you push air into it. The air is squashed into a small space. Squashed or **compressed** air is very strong.

**You will need:** two thin books, large plastic bag, a straw.

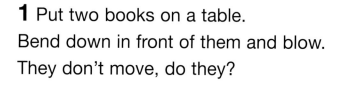

**1** Put two books on a table. Bend down in front of them and blow. They don't move, do they?

**2** Put the books on a large plastic bag on a table.

**3** Gather up the opening of the bag and tie it loosely with string. Push a straw into the hole, then blow through the straw into the bag. What is lifting the books? It is compressed air.

# Float away

Let's see which **parachute** takes the longest time to fall.

**You will need:** newspaper, large sheet of plastic, round-ended scissors, string, sticky tape, small beads, chair.

**1** Cut out two large newspaper and plastic circles.

**2** Cut six pieces of string 20cm/8in long. Tape them round the edge of a paper circle. Tie a small bead to the other ends of the strings. Tie the beads together. Do the same with a plastic circle.

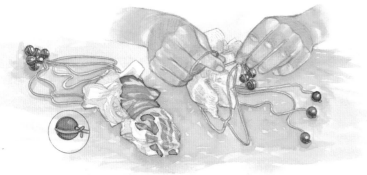

**3** Crumple the other two circles into balls. Attach strings and beads in the same way.

**4** Carefully stand on a chair. Drop two parachutes at the same time from the same height. Which parachute takes the longest time to fall? It should be the plastic parachute shaped like an umbrella.

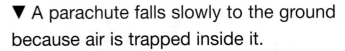

▼ A parachute falls slowly to the ground because air is trapped inside it.

# Windy weather

When air moves outside it makes the **wind**. The wind can blow from any place. It can blow hard or gently.

Look at this picture. What is causing the streamers to move? Is the wind blowing hard?

**For the next project, you will need:** washable felt-tipped pen, four sticky labels, clean yogurt pot, a pin to make a hole in the bottom of the yogurt pot, thin stick, sticky tape, plastic tray, thin cardboard, round-ended scissors, ruler, old pen lid, chair, a compass to find where north is.

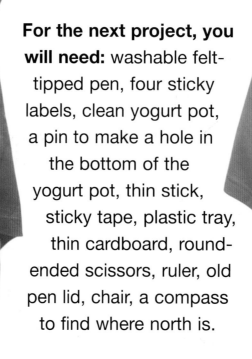

# Which way?

We can make a wind vane to find out which way the wind is blowing.

**1** Draw a cross on top of a yogurt pot. Write N, S, E and W on four sticky labels. Stick them on your pot at the ends of the cross.

**2** Make a hole through the middle of the cross. Push in a thin stick. Make sure it is upright. Tape the pot to a plastic tray.

**3** Draw an arrow on thin cardboard. Cut it out. Tape it to the top of an old pen lid. Make sure the arrow is straight.

**4** Put the arrow holder on top of the stick. Make sure it can turn easily.

**5** Take your wind vane outside. Put it on a chair. Use a compass to find where north is. Put your wind vane so that the N is pointing north. Does the arrow move when it is windy?

The arrow points in the direction the wind is blowing. So a southerly wind makes the arrow point northwards.

# Wind power

The wind can be caught and used to push things, like boats. It can drive machines such as windmills.

**You will need:** paper, round-ended scissors, straws, sticky tape, non-hardening clay, small plastic box or lid, bowl, water, pin, thin cardboard 20cm/8in square, ruler, pencil, four sticky stars, small beads, stiff plastic-covered wire.

## Sail away

**1** Cut a square of paper. Tape it to one end of a straw. This is your sail.

**2** Put some clay on the other end of the straw.

**3** Fix the sail to the middle of a small plastic box or lid. Press the clay down hard.

**4** Put your boat into a bowl of water. Blow gently into the sail. What happens? The boat is pushed along. Try larger and smaller sails. Which make the boat sail best?

# Windmill

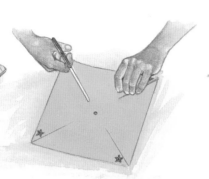

**1** Use a pin to make a hole in the middle of the cardboard. Draw lines from the corners almost to the middle. Cut along the lines. Put stars in the corners of your card as shown.

**2** Ask a grown-up to help you. Make a hole in each star. Fold these corners into the middle. They should overlap.

**3** Push a bead on to a piece of stiff, plastic-covered wire. Bend the wire over the bead. Twist the ends together.

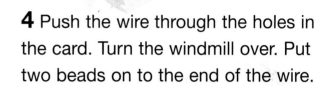

**4** Push the wire through the holes in the card. Turn the windmill over. Put two beads on to the end of the wire.

**5** Using the pin, make a hole near the top of a straw. Push the wire through the hole. Make sure the wire is straight.

**6** Make sure the windmill can turn. Twist the wire tightly round the straw.

Gently blow on the windmill. What happens? The wind makes the windmill spin.

# Hints to helpers

## Pages 6 and 7

Discuss why you can feel moving air and not still air. The still air is pressing evenly on your body. Many solid things have air trapped inside them. Try putting a handful of soil into water and watch the bubbles come out. Put a small unbaked clay brick in water and see the air bubbles rise. Leave a glass of water and see the bubbles gather on the inside of the glass.

## Page 9

It is very important that the balloons weigh the same. One balloon should be blown up as much as possible and stuck back in the same place. You could ask what would happen if the balloon was burst. Discuss where the air would go and what would happen to the stick. Burst the balloon to confirm that the weight of the balloon was due to the air and that the stick would balance again and lie level.

## Pages 10 and 11

The sheet of paper should be large, as shown in the photograph. The ruler should be hit sharply but not too hard. (If you press down on the ruler, it will act as a lever and lift the paper up.) Most children expect the paper to fly into the air, but the air pressing down on the paper stops the paper and ruler from moving.

The clear film must be tightly stretched over the top of the glass to make a flexible membrane. When the atmospheric pressure is high, the outside air presses down harder on the clear film, so the clear film dips down and the pointer rises. When the air pressure is lower, the outside air does not press down as much on the clear film. The air inside the glass pushes the clear film up, so the pointer goes down. The cardboard rule should have divisions at intervals of 1mm/$\frac{1}{16}$in either side of 0. The movement of the marker will be very slight.

## Pages 12 and 13

Look at pictures of hot-air balloons and birds circling in thermals. Discuss how the hot air rising is used to help hot-air balloons, gliders and birds rise into the air.

## Pages 14 and 15

Discuss how we use insulation in the home, such as double glazing and cavity wall insulation. Talk about warm clothes in cold weather and how it is better to wear two or three layers of clothes with air trapped in between than one very thick layer. Discuss why duvets, which have lots of air trapped in them, keep you warm in bed.

## Pages 16 and 17

Moving air has less pushing power than still air. So when you blow beneath the paper instead of flying away, the paper dips down because the air pressure on top is pushing it down.

Similarly, the air moving between the bricks has less pushing power than the still air at the side of the bricks, so the still air pushes the bricks together.

The same effect is seen in cyclones and whirlwinds. The air pressure in the middle is lower than the air pressure outside the cyclone. Therefore objects in the high pressure area are pushed into the low pressure area in the moving column of air.

## Pages 18 and 19

The air moves faster over the curved top surface of the paper wing than beneath the wing.

The air pressure above the wing is lower and has less pushing power. The higher air pressure below the paper wing pushes it up into the air. The straight wing does not rise up when you blow. Air flows over and beneath the wing at the same speed. The air pressure above and beneath the wing is equal, so the wing does not rise up.

## Pages 20 and 21

Discuss the shape of aircraft and gliders. Look at pictures of the first aircraft and fast-flying planes such as jets. Compare them with the shape of the dart.

Discuss how you could make the dart fly better – for example, by bending the wings up. Try out different sizes of dart with longer and shorter wings. Try a different dart shape, such as one with a long nose.

## Pages 22 and 23

Explain that although the model plane is much smaller than a real full-size aircraft, it flies in exactly the same way. The control surfaces on the wings and the tail of a model plane or real aircraft work by changing the way in which air flows over the aircraft. This allows the pilot to steer the aircraft in different directions. Working together, the rudder and movable flaps called ailerons on the rear edge of each wing make the plane turn to the left or right. Moving flaps called elevators on the tail make the nose of the plane go up or down. The flight of any plane is very sensitive to the angle of the controls. They need to be only a slight angle from their flat position to make the plane turn. Too big an angle will make the model unstable.

## Page 25

When a parachute falls, air is trapped and compressed inside the bell shape. The air pressure inside the parachute is higher and pushes it up. The push is not great enough to overcome the pull of gravity, but it is enough to slow the fall of the parachute. Try making different shaped parachutes and see which one takes the longest time to fall.

## Pages 26 and 27

Explain the positions of north, south, east and west on a compass. Discuss windy weather and how the wind moves at different speeds. Winds blow from areas of high air pressure to areas of low pressure. Very strong winds and hurricanes are caused by a great difference in air pressure. Winds are always given as the direction they come from, so a northerly wind is blowing from the north to the south. Look at books on the weather. Talk about weather forecasts and wind direction. For example, in winter south-westerly winds often bring rain while easterly winds often bring cold, fine weather or snow.

## Pages 28 and 29

Look at pictures of windmills and boats. Discuss how the shape of the sails helps to catch the wind. Make a simple boat and try different shaped sails. See which work best and make the boat move fastest when you sail them.

# Glossary

**Air pressure** This is the pressure of the air all around us. It presses down on everything on Earth. You cannot usually feel this pressure on you. This is because there is equal air pressure inside your body pushing outwards.

**Compressed** This means that something is squashed into a small space. When air is compressed it is very powerful. For example, compressed air is strong enough to power drills that break up concrete.

**Contracts** Gets smaller. Lots of things such as air and metal contract when they are cooled.

**Cyclone** A weather system in which a rapid inward circulation of air builds around a low-pressure central point, or eye. It is usually accompanied by stormy, often destructive weather. The term is also used more generally to mean any violent rotating windstorm.

**Deflates** Gets smaller as gas or fluid is released. A blown-up balloon deflates when you let air out of it.

**Expands** Swells out or increases in size. Lots of things such as air, metal and water expand when they are warmed.

**Gravity** The pulling force that draws objects towards the core of the Earth. Gravity keeps everything on Earth from flying off into space. It also makes objects have a weight.

**Inflates** Gets bigger by being filled with gas or fluid. A balloon inflates when you blow or pump air into it.

**Insulation** A layer of material around an object that heat cannot pass through easily. It keeps the object hot or cold for longer.

**Parachute** A large piece of fabric attached to strings that can be worn by a person. It slows down the fall of the person jumping from an aircraft.

**Streamlined** A smooth shape that allows air or a liquid to flow around it easily.

**Weather** The day-to-day temperature (if it's hot or cold), rain, cloud and wind in a place.

**Wind** Air that flows from areas of high air pressure to areas of low air pressure.

# Zimmer Gunsul Frasca Partnership

First published in the United States of America by Edizioni Press, Inc.
469 West 21st Street New York, New York 10011 Mail@edizionipress.com

ISBN: 1-931536-01-5
Library of Congress Catalogue Card Number: 2001089239
Printed in Italy
Design and Composition: Claudia Brandenburg
Editorial Director: Anthony Iannacci
Assistant Editor: Jamie Schwartz
Editorial Assistants: Kara Janeczko, Aaron Seward
Cover: Eckert and Eckert

# Building The Doernbecher Children's Hospital

# Foreword
# by Sara Hart

Healthcare in the 21st century will be appraised in terms of cost and quality, as any other consumer product or service. This industry must respond to market forces in order to survive. Medical care and the physical environment in which it's given is increasingly complex, and the soaring costs of healthcare, Medicare cuts, and bottom line-focused health maintenance organizations have created a fiercely competitive marketplace. Public institutions compete with private clinics by branding themselves as centers of premium, often specialized care. Furthermore, advances in medical technology have allowed a resource-conserving shift from inpatient to outpatient treatment. Research and development have yielded improved diagnostic tools, better medications, ambulatory oncological and surgical services, and rehabilitation care, which have reduced and, in some cases, eliminated lengthy hospital stays.

The competitive nature of providers, coupled with a discerning public, has raised expectations of healthcare environments. Until recently, most healthcare architecture served complex programming and technological requirements rather than environmental aesthetics. Following World War II, the preferred hospitals tended to be bloated regional behemoths with as many as 1,000 beds shoehorned in pairs into identical rooms on double-loaded corridors and rendered in bland modernism. By the 1980s and 90s, healthcare advocates began to question the impersonal, warehouse feeling of these anonymous settings, suggesting that they might actually inhibit patient response to treatment. Eventually, behavioral research confirmed that hospitals designed for patient well-being, instead of healthcare-provider convenience, promote healing—an unexpected conclusion in a streamlined, technologically driven system. All of these factors have turned passive and vulnerable patients into savvy healthcare consumers, driven by both desire and necessity to participate in their own care and treatment.

Family-centered care is most poignantly observed in the treatment of sick children. Doernbecher Children's Hospital at the Oregon Health Sciences University in Portland, Oregon, is an interesting hybrid of a large regional institution serving five states and an intimate family-centered hospital funded for the most part at the local level. Designed by Zimmer Gunsul Frasca Partnership (ZGF), Doernbecher is a model of programmatic and design harmony. The architect's role as designer of an institutional envelope that encloses high-tech machinery and centralized operations has been transformed to creator of a highly integrated and meticulously detailed synthesis of form and function, scale and texture, art and adornment.

ZGF crafted three residentially scaled courtyards to soften Doernbecher's monolithic massing. These are reminiscent of the courtyard hospitals of the 19th and early 20th centuries, which encouraged a relationship to nature, natural light, and fresh air. The 80-bed nursing units surround the courtyards and are laced with homey amenities to relieve the stress of both patients and their families. Although Doernbecher's extensive outpatient services reflect current trends in healthcare, ZGF has reinvented the clinic as a public gathering place with non-institutional amenities and diversions.

The atmosphere at Doernbecher is one of healing, not sickness. With the comfort of their families provided for, patients convalesce in a supportive environment free from the arid repetition associated with medical centers of the past. ZGF has made Doernbecher the architectural paradigm for healthcare environments of the 21st century.

# Building The Doernbecher Children's Hospital

Dr. Ron Rosenfeld had spent 25 years at Stanford University when Dr. Peter Kohler, president of Oregon Health Sciences University (OHSU), asked him to consider accepting the chairmanship for the Department of Pediatrics and position of physician-in-chief for Doernbecher Children's Hospital, located in Portland, on the OHSU campus. Rosenfeld's decision was influenced by Doernbecher's prestigious history.

Since 1926, Doernbecher Children's Hospital has provided comprehensive pediatric care for the region, especially for children in rural areas. As members of the OHSU system, Doernbecher's clinical researchers pioneered innovations in microsurgery and opened the nation's first academic children's eye clinic in 1949. In the 1950s, Doernbecher treated children with polio, opened the Child Development and Rehabilitation Center (CDRC), and performed Oregon's first pediatric open-heart surgery and the state's first pediatric kidney transplant (the tenth in the world). In 1968, Doernbecher developed the state's first neonatal intensive care center.

By the 1990s, when Rosenfeld was considering Kohler's proposition, advanced research continued at OHSU in all areas of pediatric medicine, especially treatment therapies for cancer and organ transplants. As part of OHSU's interdisciplinary system of academic and research facilities, the hospital was a renowned success. Every year, more than 30,000 children and adolescents from Oregon and five surrounding states receive treatment at Doernbecher. This figure includes the 7,500 children who are served by the CDRC's diagnostic, treatment, and rehabilitation facilities. Embracing the enormous possibilities, Rosenfeld accepted the position and came to Portland.

Rosenfeld weighed both the benefits and the problems. "On the one hand, pediatrics was under-served. The facilities were totally inadequate, housed on two floors of OHSU Hospital with two to four children per room and only one bathroom per floor," explains Rosenfeld. Since 1956, Doernbecher had occupied the top three floors of the OHSU Hospital. As its services expanded, so did patient volume. Outpatient and other services were quickly crowded out of the hospital and relegated to different locations across the sprawling campus. Due to overcrowding, any privacy for parents and family members had been virtually eliminated. "On the other

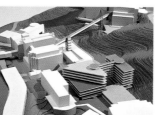  

FAR LEFT: This view of the site, which looks back toward OHSU Hospital, shows the U.S. Veterans Administration Hospital. LEFT: This view of the site shows the existing parking structure and the U.S. Veterans Administration Hospital pedestrian bridge. BELOW: ZGF presented a variety of conceptual ideas during the architect selection process to demonstrate the design team's understanding of the complex issues related to accommodating the hospital's programmatic requirements on the constricted, hilltop campus. FOLLOWING PAGE: ZGF explored a number of alternatives to test the building massing, campus connections, public access, and costs associated with potential sites.

hand," continues Rosenfeld, "there was a commitment to upgrade the facility; yet even in these overcrowded conditions, Doernbecher had the best reputation of any hospital in the state. There was great potential. I thought Doernbecher should be the jewel in the crown of OHSU. All the components were in place: a major medical school, strong research, and excellent obstetrics."

In 1994, it was decided to build a new hospital somewhere on the densely built OHSU campus, atop Marquam Hill. The new facility was to replace and expand previously dispersed pediatric inpatient and ambulatory care, diagnostic evaluation and treatment, education, and administrative and public services. Rosenfeld led the development of Doernbecher's new home.

After a public call for qualifications, Rosenfeld and the Doernbecher team invited a short list of architects to formal interviews. At this time, Zimmer Gunsul Frasca Partnership (ZGF) responded with a team of consultants, which included KPFF Consulting Engineers and Anshen + Allen as associate architect responsible for medical planning and programming. Doernbecher retained ZGF, and the team it had assembled, to design the new hospital.

Rosenfeld worked closely with faculty and staff to create a new facility for the hospital,

"I remember our first design meetings when Bob Frasca began sharing some of his visions. We made it clear from the onset that winning design awards was not our goal; our primary concerns were creating a building that functioned well, and had a good feeling. The fact that we were able to combine award-winning design with functionality and an environment that actually feels good is a true measure of the genius of the architect." Susanne Banz, Administrator, Doernbecher Children's Hospital

developing a close relationship with the architects, and specifically with partner Robert Frasca. "Bob was flexible and approachable. He came to meetings and challenged our assumptions," says Rosenfeld.

After four years of challenge, compromise, and bold, forward-looking design, Doernbecher Children's Hospital opened its doors in July 1998 to grateful children and their families, and received much acclaim. The new hospital is an 80-bed, 250,000-square-foot pediatric facility with a 75-year history of medical innovation and quality patient care.

"It's never easy being in a hospital, but you've thought about us and what we need; you can tell you listened to families," said a father of a 6-month-old baby hospitalized for respiratory distress.

## Family-Centered Care

This was not to be just another children's hospital with perfunctory, albeit high quality, services and treatment. The notion of family-centered care informed all the planning for this new facility. Family-centered care is an approach that starts with the fundamental belief that emotional support is critical to healing. Family members are not just visitors; they are partners in the

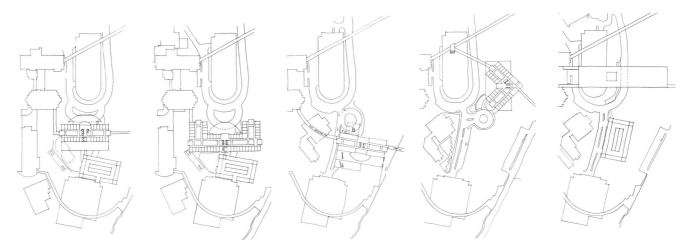

delivery of healthcare to their loved ones. Family-centered principles are not "applied" after the building is designed. Rather, patients, families, physicians, nurses, and administrators are immersed in the design process from the outset. This is particularly true in a pediatric environment.

At Doernbecher, all parties adopted a holistic mantra: If a child is ill, the whole family needs to participate. Every service, every space was designed to meet the needs of the children and their families. ZGF brought together physicians, nurses, and support staff to document their medical and procedural requirements. Then parents and their children, who had suffered life-threatening diseases and injuries, were invited to participate. By relating their experiences, these concerned parents identified often overlooked but otherwise basic amenities that make a traumatic experience bearable. Three major planning sessions were conducted. These provided an opportunity for families to review design ideas, as well as other informal opportunities to verify design assumptions. As a result, privacy and a semblance of domestic familiarity became the paramount design intent for the hospital.

"The overarching sense is one of CARING; we cared enough to design and build a facility to support children and their families; we cared enough to listen to their ideas and use them; we cared enough to put that caring into the physical structures and spaces and it shows to our families and to our staff. We are more nurturing and supportive because of the beauty of our environment." Susie Bacon, RN, MPA: HA, Family and Services Coordinator, Doernbecher Children's Hospital

## A Fundraising Feat

OHSU estimated that it would cost about $60 million to build a new hospital. The formulation of the budget and the development of a funding strategy were joint efforts between the Doernbecher Foundation, the fundraising arm of the hospital, and OHSU. They decided on a strategy, whereby they would raise the money from construction bonds and private donations. The Foundation had hired John Stuart May as its executive director in 1992. Under his direction, gifts to the hospital increased by 500 percent, to about $9 million annually. For the new hospital's capital campaign, the Foundation relied not only on traditional fundraising strategies, like black-tie charity events, but also adopted an aggressive, ecumenical strategy to pull in untapped resources. They attracted support from every demographic, from school children to local and regional businesses.

The grassroots efforts were enormously successful. A dozen volunteer chapters, the Friends of Doernbecher, raised both awareness for the campaign and $2 million from their neighbors by sponsoring golf tournaments, concerts, fashion shows, and holiday card sales. Credit union employees in Oregon and southwest Washington raised $1.7 million by selling cookbooks, Christmas trees, and cookies to their members.

The fundraising project that reached individuals at every economic level was the sale of 8,000 personalized bricks to be used as pavers in the facility's walkways and courtyards. Every brick is engraved with

The design team used early schematic massing models to study the impact of the desired building configuration, connections, and fit within the campus context. They also explored the concept of interior courtyards.

the donor's name at a cost of $144. This odd figure allows individuals to finance their donation over a year at a manageable $12 a month. The ongoing brick campaign has raised $1.2 million to date. The central courtyard and the entry into the hospital lobby are paved with these engraved bricks donated by thousands of citizens. Maps obtained at the registration desk locate each brick by the donor's name, thus drawing the community to these areas and reinforcing a sense of ownership that fosters continuing donor participation and support.

Traditional philanthropists came through as well. The Ford family, owners of Roseburg Forest Products, gave a generous $3.1 million. Paul Allen, Microsoft cofounder and owner of the Portland Trailblazers, gave $1 million, as did the Kresge Foundation and many others.

A parallel campaign was instituted to solicit in-kind donations of supplies, equipment, and building materials. By the end of construction, 32 companies had donated $2 million worth of products, not the least of which was a major donation of steel for the structure by Portland-based Oregon Steel Mills and American Steel. Construction companies and suppliers contributed services and materials through the general contractor with the support of the Columbia Pacific Building Trades Council.

ZGF also played a key role in fundraising. They made a monetary contribution and raised matching funds from their consultant team. They donated presentation materials (models, computer animations, etc.) utilized in fundraising and accommodated donated materials in the design of the building. Key ZGF staff members cultivated and solicited major gifts.

"This project moved all of us. It can be appreciated by both kids and adults; it's fresh and uplifting and the artwork is well-integrated with the architecture."
1998 IIDA/AIA/ASID Interior Design Awards Jury, Portland Chapter

## A Fund for Art

A donation that had a dramatic influence on the new hospital came from a Portland family that made an anonymous $600,000 contribution in memory of their daughter, to fund art installations throughout the building. "Our daughter believed in the power of art to heal and give meaning to life and death." In memory of her "and all sons and daughters," the family committed to making the new children's hospital "a lively, joyful and welcoming place through art."

This clear and sweeping vision became the foundation for the art program, which was managed by Eloise Damrosch, public art director for Portland's Regional Arts & Culture Council. The Doernbecher Hospital Art Committee was formed, chaired by a Portland citizen and composed of OHSU and hospital

LEFT: The new building presents a compelling image from many vantage points. A significant design goal was to create a uniquely identifiable institution through the approach and entry sequence.
BELOW: This rendering illustrates the structures that support the building. The south end of the hospital is built into a small ravine in the hillside. The next northerly support is the central building core, founded on high-capacity drilled concrete piling. The three remaining supports consist of a cast-in-place concrete bent and two new bearing walls, which pass through the existing parking structure.

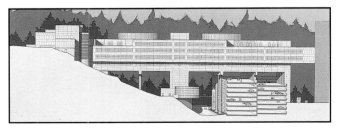

staff, artists, and the architects. The committee's charge was to identify meaningful places throughout the hospital where art could be integrated, and to select the artists and their work. A nationwide "Call to Artists" attracted over 500 applicants, from which seven artists and artist teams were ultimately chosen.

The seamless integration of art and architecture represents one of the most extraordinary aspects of the entire project. At an orientation meeting for the artists, the vision of the donor was shared and the tone was set. Everyone also agreed that because a pediatric hospital treats patients ranging in age from newborn to 18 years, and accommodates their families, the art had to appeal to children and adults of all ages.

## The Building as Bridge

When ZGF was awarded the commission, they had a project with no site. The 32-building OHSU campus sprawls across 116 acres on scenic Marquam Hill, a sloping, wooded area southwest of downtown Portland with views of Mount Hood. An enormous 500-foot-wide ravine bisects the hill, sloping at 45 degrees from the north and south faces to a depth of 100 feet. With this formidable canyon occupying so much of the hill, there were very few sites left on which to build such a large complex.

Doernbecher received permission from the state to bypass the mandatory competitive bidding process required for public projects and adopt the private-sector method of negotiating a contract with the general contractor and construction manager up front. After reviewing several submissions, OHSU chose Hoffman Construction Company, a 79-year-old full-service firm, to act as both general contractor and construction manager.

First, OHSU negotiated a guaranteed maximum price (GMP) with Hoffman; then the team went in search of a buildable site. They investigated razing some existing buildings to free-up a site, while relocating the displaced functions elsewhere. This proposal created another set of logistical problems and was quickly abandoned. Finally, they began to explore the seemingly unbuildable canyon. First, they considered the possibility of building into one side of the canyon. This proved too expensive, and, more importantly, it failed to connect OHSU Hospital on the north ridge to the CDRC on the south. In addition, the portion of the building buried in the hillside would be without natural light, an unacceptable compromise.

Then Rosenfeld suggested building across the canyon. If the hospital stretched from the CDRC to OHSU Hospital, vital connections could be made to existing neonatal, MRI, food preparation, and emergency facilities, thus eliminating costly redundancies. The concept of "building-as-bridge" surfaced immediately. Spanning the ravine offered a dramatic design solution.

## The Challenges of Construction

From a construction standpoint, such a long span required steel members too long to be transported on the narrow winding roads leading to

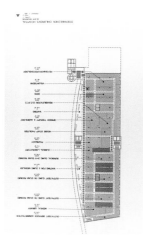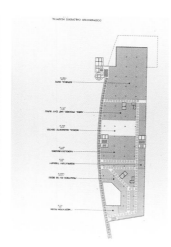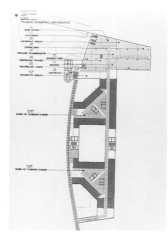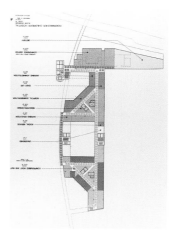

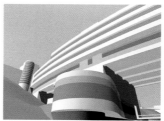

ABOVE: Blocking and stacking diagrams illustrate how programs for Levels 7 through 10 (LEFT TO RIGHT) were carefully crafted into a building. Programmatic adjacencies and desired connections to adjacent buildings drove the architecture of the building. LEFT: A three-dimensional computer animation, developed for Doernbecher's fundraising efforts, displayed the dynamic building design to potential donors.

the site. The team determined that it would be too difficult to truck in any steel member longer than 45 feet. On-site fabrication in the steep ravine was considered too impractical. The ravine also precluded the erection of scaffolding. Access to the site was limited by an existing eight-story parking structure at the northern end of the site, and by two separate portions of a busy street located directly under the new structure.

Faced with these challenges, the contractor and engineers from KPFF Consulting Engineers selected a system of long-span steel plate girders with intermediate supports placed at six strategic locations: three to the south, and three to north of S.W. Sam Jackson Park Road. This allowed the girders to be lifted into place by a 308-ton crane, the largest crane in the Northwest, which could be moved to hoist the structural members from limited locations. These girders formed a platform, as high as 100 feet above the ground, on which to construct a "conventional" hospital structure. The depth of the girders forms an interstitial space to provide services to all areas of the hospital.

The south end of the hospital is built into a small ravine in the hillside. Hoffman excavated and infilled portions of the ravine to provide a series of terraced benches that support the building foundations. A three-column, cast-in-place concrete bent, along with the central building core, serves as the structural support

system for the south side of the building. Clad at the base in ashlar sandstone from Idaho, the central core contains the entrance lobby and various types of mechanical equipment. Like each of the supports, it is founded on high-capacity drilled concrete piling. Two hundred rock anchors were installed 60 feet into the hillside bedrock to stabilize the hillside and resist seismic forces. The piling and rock anchors served a dual purpose by also retaining the hillside to the south as the site was excavated.

The three remaining supports for the hospital consist of a cast-in-place concrete bent directly south of the parking structure, and two new bearing walls constructed through the existing garage. These walls extend approximately 25 feet above the upper parking deck. The hospital mandated that the garage stay open throughout the construction process, and that no more than 35 stalls be removed from public use, making the scheduling and construction of these walls and their foundations critical. Although the concept was based on a steel truss system, the team later replaced the trusses with steel plate girders after Oregon Steel Mills and American Steel offered materials for the girders as an in-kind donation. Five rows of 8-foot, 4-inch-deep plate girders span the ravine between the supports. These were erected in 45-foot lengths as cantilevers off the supports. The sections between the cantilevers were then infilled with comparable girders that were bolted into place, as field welding was impractical 100 feet in the air. Once erection of the girders was complete, precast concrete planks were

"The building as a 'bridge' allows the design to exhibit a strong feeling of lightness, which obscures the scale and makes for a more approachable building. It is well integrated into the landscape. It's a sophisticated environment with the most original artwork and signals systems that I have seen in a children's facility." 1999 Modern Healthcare Awards Jury

Faced with many challenges, the architectural, engineering and contracting team used a system of long-span steel plate girders with intermediate supports placed at six strategic locations on the canyon floor. The girders, lifted into place by a large crane, formed a platform as high as 100 feet above the ground, on which construction of a "conventional" structure could begin.

installed between the lower flanges of adjacent girders to form the floor of the interstitial level. As Bill Forsythe, Hoffman's project manager, explains, "Once the planks were in place, construction of the hospital floors was fairly conventional." The building frame consists of composite steel beams and girders and steel columns, which support the 55,000-square-foot floor plates. The building frame above the girder level was erected using two tower cranes, one adjacent to the parking garage, and the other within a freight elevator shaft at the south end of the building.

## Critical Connections

"The organization of the building grew out of the vital physical connections to OHSU Hospital and the CDRC, as well as the site constraints," explains Karl Sonnenberg, the ZGF partner involved in medical planning. It was important that Doernbecher's floors and floor numbers correspond with OHSU Hospital, given that Doernbecher relies on OHSU Hospital for certain specialty services. Direct physical connections are made on two levels. Horizontal relationships were equally important. The architects organized the building so that the most actively visited floors are on the lowest levels, reserving the upper floors for more sensitive areas, such as oncology. The main entry and public lobby are accessed at Level 3 of the central building core.

Level 7, the first of four full floors of the new hospital, houses outpatient clinics, a pharmacy, a lab, and the radiology and rehabilitation departments. These functions are grouped on this floor, closest to the lobby, and separated from inpatient functions on the levels above. The public circulation spine here (and on all patient floors above) follows the curve of the east façade, which orients visitors by providing sweeping views of Portland and the Cascade Mountains beyond.

Level 8 holds critical functions, including a 16-bed Pediatric Intensive Care Unit (PICU) and operating rooms. This level connects to OHSU Hospital so children can be transported from that facility's emergency room to Doernbecher's PICU or surgery without taking an elevator. All patient, staff and service traffic connects to OHSU Hospital at this level.

Level 9, which houses two 24-bed inpatient nursing units for adolescents and young children respectively, provides a public connection to OHSU Hospital's main lobby level. The cancer center is located on Level 10, reducing exposure for the immune-compromised patients receiving inpatient care. A partial floor at the south end of the building, Level 11 houses the Joseph Vey Conference Center, a 150-seat auditorium and meeting facility used for seminars, staff meetings, and public events.

"We gave a lot of thought to the inter-relationships between various operational pieces of the hospital. The patient flow and departmental relationships work extremely well. We knew going in that when the time came to expand, some of this efficiency may be compromised—that the location of the building would pose challenges. Altogether, the predicament posed by the need to expand is a desirable one; it's a testament to our success, our original planning, and the innovative design. I have no doubt we will come up with a solution that will work equally well." Susanne Banz, Administrator, Doernbecher Children's Hospital

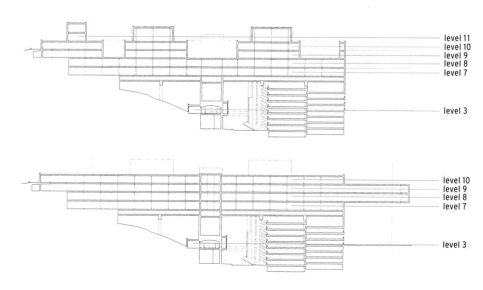

level 11
level 10
level 9
level 8
level 7

level 3

level 10
level 9
level 8
level 7

level 3

Building sections illustrate placement of intimate courtyards that bring daylight into the patient rooms (TOP) and show critical horizontal and vertical programmatic relationships (BOTTOM), including connections to OHSU Hospital at Levels 8 and 9.

During the planning and design process, the team considered options for future expansion. The intent always was to add another nursing unit on Level 10, which would involve relocating clinical and administrative facilities. Building a new wing into the hillside at the south end was determined as the preferred alternative. As the hospital's needs grew and changed over the last few years, other possibilities have been explored, including an expansion of two new levels south at the core leg of the building.

## The Architecture Unfolds

As programmatic adjacencies were being planned, ZGF architects were developing the massing and designing the envelope, seeking ways to bring daylight into the interior cores to give the large medical facility a more familiar, even residential, scale.

Frasca envisioned a building envelope that had the grace of an ocean liner sailing through the treetops. Such imagery seemed conducive to healing, a hospital floating rather than looming. The ocean liner imagery is most obvious in the gently curving east façade, which levitates dramatically across the thickly vegetated gorge. This is the first image visitors see as they wind up S.W. Sam Jackson Park Road, pass under the building, circle 180 degrees, and follow the drive to the lobby entrance. Still, a significant challenge was determining how to bring natural light into a mass that was 500 feet long and 150 feet deep. During the schematic design phase, ZGF explored carving out two, and finally settled on three, interior open courtyards in the center of the building, thus allowing daylight to filter into patient rooms on the two upper levels.

With the massing determined, the architects turned their attention to cladding. Although a brick vernacular pervades the OHSU campus, ZGF searched for a light-weight, low-maintenance surface material appropriate for a building that is perched 100 feet in the air. Repairing or cleaning this area would be extremely difficult, especially if a panel system with wet sealants—which require periodic replacement and often produce streaks on the panels during the Northwest's rainy season—was used. Instead, they specified a dry-gasket, aluminum-panel, curtain wall system similar to the cladding of the nearby Casey Eye Institute. The system's 4-foot by 20-foot white panels create a subtle, rational grid, modulated by square, etched windows and projections on both the east and west façades.

When it came to articulating the interior courtyards, however, ZGF adopted an altogether different architectural vocabulary. Frasca's inspiration came from a photograph of a small French hotel featuring a courtyard with vine-covered trellises. In this image he saw an opportunity to pursue a warm, non-urban treatment for these outdoor spaces. Each courtyard is expressed in a slightly different manner, but the façades are all finished in stucco and the windows are all shaded by fabric awnings. Because the courtyard façades and the metal-clad perimeter façades are never juxtaposed,

BELOW LEFT: The internal courtyards, shown here under construction, bring personality and scale to the large structure. The drum-shaped mechanical penthouses were designed to maximize natural light in the courtyard spaces.

BELOW RIGHT: In addition to providing an overview of the building exterior and its placement on the OHSU campus, the computer animation offered a virtual tour of the central interior courtyard spaces.

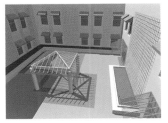

there's no conflict between the radically different scales, finish materials, and articulation.

The south courtyard, painted soft green, is called the "quiet courtyard," and is used by families and visitors. The central rose-colored courtyard has a gazebo, a fountain, and play equipment, all designed by artist Wayne Chabre, for use by patients and their visiting siblings and friends. The yellow-toned north courtyard provides outdoor seating for hospital staff.

## Humanizing the Interiors

ZGF was asked by OHSU to develop an overall theme for the interior design of the new hospital. Doernbecher administrators and staff directed the design team to create an interior environment that appeals to the child in all of us. Inspiration came from the building's site, nestled amongst the trees, and the magnificence of Portland's largely unspoiled natural surroundings. For the interiors, the designers pursued imagery based on the natural world. Everyone agreed that this direction was appropriate; it was in sync with the art program, and could be articulated to appeal to patients who range widely in age, without being patronizing.

Themes of nature were developed for each of the four patient floors (Levels 7 through 10): "Animal World"; "Flora and Fauna"; "Earth and Sky"; and "Sea and Shore." Imagery based on these themes percolates through all the artwork and details, giving the

*"You really thought about what we need," said the mother of an 8-year-old surgery patient, whose 3- and 4-year-old siblings were playing in the rose-colored play courtyard.*

whole interior scheme a refinement not generally seen in institutional environments.

In a hospital for children, color, pattern, and texture are as much science as art. Colors should be cheerful, but not so saturated that they become dark and potentially ominous at night or on cloudy days. In an area of the country that sees the sun go down at mid-afternoon in winter, artificial lighting and surface treatments become important psychological factors in creating a comforting atmosphere. Jan Crider, Doernbecher's child-life therapist, worked with ZGF's interiors team, led by Sharron van der Meulen and Terri Johnson, providing input into the psychological connotations of animal shapes, textures, and colors. From the moment families enter the lobby until they sit down in a patient's private room, the combination of color, art, light, scale, and proportion creates a warm, supportive environment.

The interiors team also focused a great deal of energy on signage and way-finding. "Many patients and their families may not speak English as their first language," explains van der Meulen. "We worked with a signage consultant, Anderson Krygier, Inc., to create an international language based on images

The interiors team worked with consultant Anderson Krygier, Inc., to develop a signage program based on icons from nature, since many patients and their families may not speak English as their first language. The graphics, chosen to identify various departments within the hospital, work in concert with the themes of nature developed for each patient floor: "Animal World"; "Flora and Fauna"; "Earth and Sky"; and "Sea and Shore."

rather than numbers and words, one that would be fun for children." Plant and animal graphics were chosen to identify various departments. They all had to be soft and round, without sharp edges or bared teeth.

Distinctions between departments are also emphasized by accent colors, which are used as way-finding devices. For instance, the color of the linoleum applied to the vertical surfaces at each reception desk defines the color used throughout the department. This same color continues onto the floors of examination or treatment rooms and around the doors, creating a subconscious continuity of color that leads a patient clearly through the space from the moment of arrival.

The sense of scale also has an impact on the interior environment. With a move that accommodates all, desk heights are varied and countertops gracefully slope from adult-standing height at the rounded corners down to sitting or child height in the middle. Overall attention to scale results in both visual and physical accessibility to services and people, and creates a communal atmosphere.

The themes of nature are carried throughout the public spaces and patient rooms in numerous ways. For example, playful imagery of plant and animal life appears on ZGF custom-designed cubicle curtains, inspired by Matisse images. Stenciled wall motifs in

the exam rooms, designed by artists Jon Early and Laura Bender, complement these colors and images. Cast bronze drawer pulls denote the respective theme of each floor. Embossed acoustical ceiling tiles, arranged in constellation patterns above patient beds, further reflect the natural imagery.

One of the most delightfully animated details appears in the borders etched around the windowpanes in patient rooms and corridors. In accordance with the spirit of the art program, ZGF chose to redirect money in their architectural budget to engage artist Margot Voorhies Thompson to design this feature, which was utilized on all patient floors. Patterns formed by a white ceramic frit diffuse daylight and reflect the interior light back into the room at night. The result is a continuous play of light and shadow on the surrounding surfaces.

The curved public circulation spine on Level 7 (and on all the patient floors above) is modulated with seating areas and play sculptures. The interiors team designed castle-like casework to break down the scale of the waiting areas and house televisions, games, and aquariums. The art committee saw these areas as opportunities to include interactive artworks (for example, "Peepholes," designed by artists Fernanda D'Agostino, Valerie Otani and Elizabeth Stanek).

Because of the critical nature of the care on Level 8, the design team recognized the need for subtle variations in the public spaces. The waiting area is divided into three sections—an open seating

"The building has worked extremely well and the way it works well goes far beyond the functional aspects. Families and staff have commented that it feels so friendly—that the combination of colors and the fact that we have so much natural light creates an environment that is non-threatening. It's one of the highest compliments you can give a building that serves sick, frightened children and supports what we do." Susanne Banz, Administrator, Doernbecher Children's Hospital

The design team thoughtfully considered the psychological connotations of the texture and pattern of materials used throughout the hospital. The final materials extend the themes of nature throughout the public spaces and patient rooms. For example, playful imagery of plant and animal life appears on ZGF custom-designed cubicle curtains, inspired by Matisse images (BELOW RIGHT).

area, a partially enclosed playroom, and a fully enclosed quiet waiting room. A high-tech ICU environment can be frightening, but the Pediatric Intensive Care Unit provides a friendly atmosphere.

The courtyards are located on Level 9, which houses the acute care nursing units. Windowsills are lower than normal so small and bedridden patients can view the outdoors. The same attention to detail is evident here as on the other floors. In the spirit of family-centered care, all patient rooms are private; each has a bathroom and a built-in bed with drawers for the use of parents who want to stay with their child. Many children endure long stays, so every nursing unit is equipped with a family kitchen, a playroom for patients and siblings, and a variety of lounges for the families. A laundry facility for families is available on Level 9.

The inpatient rooms create a home in the hospital. The large square windows in patient rooms have wood frames and mullions. The hand-stenciled plant and animal motifs extend through the patient room walls and corridors. The designers also gave private baths a personalized, residential feel by randomly placing colorful, handmade tiles by artist Dana Lynn Louis.

"The architects created a seamless relationship between inside and outside. The jury was struck by the use of powerful architectural form to link disparate parts of the existing hospital campus and at the same time to establish an environment of enormous warmth and humanity for what can be a scary situation for children and their families." 1999 Portland Chapter AIA Awards Jury

"I've never seen a hospital like this one, and we've been in a LOT of them," said another mother whose family moved from out-of-state and whose daughter is medically fragile and will receive extensive care at Doernbecher.

Designers developed a strategy to make each of the nursing units, and the Kenneth W. Ford Northwest Children's Cancer Center on Level 10, a "neighborhood." Corridors become "streets," organized around the nurses' stations. "Welcome mats" at each patient room door are created by patterns in the vinyl tile. At each doorway, a space is provided for personal artwork or a family photo, reminding staff and visitors of the individuality of each patient. The result is a delicate balance between personal privacy and professional vigilance that is mutually respectful.

## Art to Inspire Healing

The integration of art played a powerful role in humanizing the environment of the hospital. The installations begin in front of the entrance. As visitors pass under the entry awning lobby, they are greeted by fanciful tactile sculptures, designed by Frank Boyden and Brad Rude. Inside the vestibule, a granite ring, nine feet in diameter, circles a large stone in the center of the floor. Various animal and human footprints are imprinted around the perimeter of the ring. Within

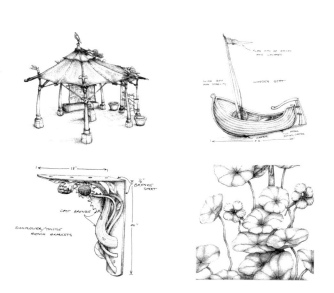
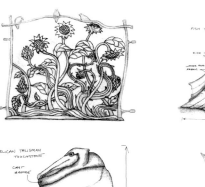
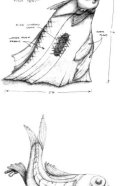

the ring, words from a poem written for Doernbecher by Portland poet Kim Stafford are inscribed: "Young friend, be home here, be healed, be well, be with us all, young friend." Other installations in the lobby, by Boyden and Rude, range from a vibrantly painted 3-foot, 5-inch-high aluminum frieze that follows the lobby's winding window wall in a pageantry of animals, plants, and other natural elements, to oversized bronze fruits and vegetables that serve as armrests along built-in perimeter seating.

Throughout the hospital, a variety of artwork in varying scales allows patients and visitors to escape from their fears for a moment. In the Level 7 waiting area, for example, children are encouraged to climb on a huge turtle sculpture, by artist Rosalie Sherman. People waiting for elevators can enjoy metal panels etched with leaf images and adorned with glass butterflies and dragonflies. Artists Suzanne Lee and Valerie Otani also created etched metal wall sconces that cast colored light across the wall. These same artists designed light boxes for the ceilings in the patient elevator lobbies to help alleviate the anxieties of children looking up from their gurneys.

Wayne Chabre created an entire environment in the children's play courtyard, using a landscape of pavers, a pavilion with animals, a fish fountain, and ceramic tiles of medicinal plants that surround the doorways. This artist also designed the "Art Carp," a playful, fish-like transporter that brings art supplies to patients throughout the hospital.

"This is a wonderfully designed facility. The atmosphere is friendly, beautiful and soothing. Portland is lucky to have such a great place for its children and their families," said the mother of a patient treated for conductive hearing loss.

"He loves coming to the clinic because he can play around here," said the parents of one long-term clinic patient.

The meditation room on Level 10, created by artists Jim Hirschfield and Sonya Ishii, provides an elegant, simple space for contemplation. Concentric, mandala-like circles of light project through a cut-out ceiling onto a pale wooden floor, while colored leaf images cut into the window project light during the day as the sun passes.

As the work of each artist unfolded, the themes of nature were woven throughout the art and interiors. It was a testament to the power of the collective vision—that Doernbecher is a place for healing. With the interiors, as with the exterior massing and articulation, the subtle layering of images, the juxtaposition of textures and colors, and sensitivity to appropriateness of scale, combine to create a whole that surpasses the sum of all the highly refined details.

"Having been involved in the planning process for the new Doernbecher, you can imagine how pleased we all were to have our already high expectations so pleasantly and so consistently exceeded. The entire medical staff shares the feeling that we have the great fortune of treating patients in a world-class facility. And I know our patients and their families are benefited every day by this extraordinary hospital." Dr. Ron Rosenfeld, Physician-in-Chief, Doernbecher Children's Hospital

PREVIOUS PAGE: Funded by an anonymous donation of $600,000, an extensive art program helped make the hospital a lively, joyful, and welcoming place. A nationwide "Call to Artists" attracted over 500 applicants, from which seven artists and artist teams were ultimately selected. These sketches, by artist Wayne Chabre, illustrate the components of his proposed installation in the rose-colored play courtyard.
THIS PAGE: Chabre also designed the "Art Carp," a playful, fish-like transporter that carries art supplies to patients throughout the hospital.

# The Building: Doernbecher Children's Hospital, OHSU Campus

The site plan (THIS PAGE) illustrates the position of the hospital (FOLLOWING PAGE) within the densely built campus. The July 1999 issue of *Architectural Record* stated, "Doernbecher Children's Hospital turned a difficult site into an asset, bridging the gap between two existing buildings on opposing hillsides and knitting together a sprawling medical complex...the hospital soars above its access road while presenting an elegant face to its neighbors."

PREVIOUS PAGE, ABOVE: There were no traditional sites available on the 32-building campus that would accommodate the new hospital. The architects first considered razing some of the existing buildings, but, due to logistical problems, the plan was abandoned. The seemingly unbuildable canyon proved to be the most logical, compelling, and economically feasible site. BELOW: The form and materials of the new children's hospital create a structure that appears to float above the treetops like an ocean liner. THIS PAGE, LEFT: By reaching across the canyon, the architects were able to link the Child Development and Rehabilitation Center and OHSU Hospital, making vital connections to the existing neonatal, ICU, MRI, and emergency facilities, thus eliminating costly redundancies. BELOW: Visitors get their first glimpse of the gently curving east façade, which dramatically levitates across the vegetated gorge, as they wind up S.W. Sam Jackson Park Road, pass under the building, circle 180 degrees, and follow the drive to the entrance plaza.

PREVIOUS PAGE AND THIS PAGE, TOP: Doernbecher required a prominent main entrance that could be easily distinguished from the other buildings on the crowded hillside campus. A cantilevered architectural element above enhances visual identification of the entry. A convenient turnaround outside the front door facilitates patient drop-off and serves as a welcoming refuge at the end of the narrow, winding road that leads to the hospital. Parking is conveniently located nearby. ABOVE, LEFT: East-West section. ABOVE, RIGHT: East elevation.

THIS PAGE, RIGHT: A lantern-like, glass-block expression of the southern stairway, which connects all levels within the building, links the hospital to the south campus. BELOW: The curving east façade effectively softens the long, linear massing of the building. FOLLOWING PAGE: The exterior panels of the upper building are contrasted by a split-face stone base, which anchors the structure into the hillside.

BELOW: As visitors pass under the canopy at the main entrance, they are greeted by welcoming tactile sculptures, designed by artists Frank Boyden and Brad Rude. FOLLOWING PAGE: Created by the same artists, a nine-foot diameter ring inside the vestibule floor was formed by black granite from Africa and blue granite from Brazil. Beyond this ring are numerous footprints of bears, herons, dogs, dinosaurs, and a human mother and child.

# Level 3

**Main Entry, Public Lobby, Registration, Family Medical Resource Library**

THIS PAGE: The main entry level and public lobby are accessed at Level 3 of the central building core. The lobby was configured to take advantage of views down the canyon and into the adjacent forested ravine.
FOLLOWING PAGE: A vibrantly painted 3-foot, 5-inch-high aluminum frieze, designed by artists Frank Boyden and Brad Rude, follows the lobby's curved window wall in a pageantry of animals, flora and fauna, and natural elements. The artists' oversized bronze fruits and vegetables serve as armrests along the built-in perimeter seating and establish whimsical focal points for children of all ages.

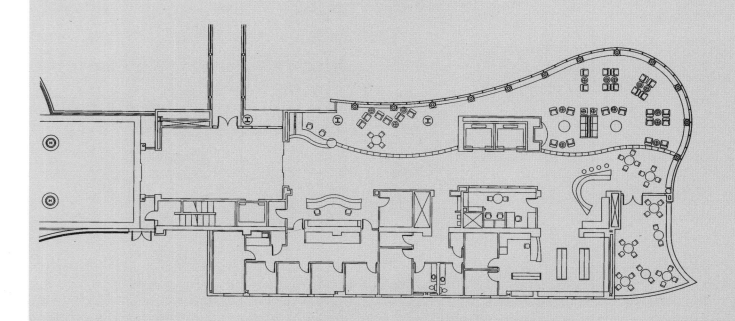

THIS PAGE, TOP, LEFT AND ABOVE: The interiors team was sensitive to scale throughout the hospital, giving careful consideration to all users of the space. Desk heights are varied and countertops slope from adult-standing height at the rounded corners down to sitting or child height in the middle. THIS PAGE, TOP, RIGHT: Stone-framed display cases in the main lobby showcase the artwork of patients. THIS PAGE, BELOW: Interior elevation of main lobby reception desk. FOLLOWING PAGE: Comfortable seating, natural lighting and a central fireplace in the main lobby create a welcoming space for families, visitors, and staff. The lobby was also configured to accommodate the hospital's special events.

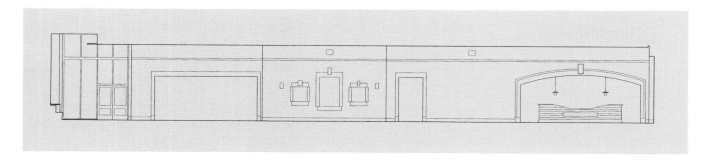

THIS PAGE, BELOW: During an orientation meeting for the chosen artists, many parties involved with the hospital—including architects, Doernbecher staff, parents of patients, and the Doernbecher Art Committee, led by Eloise Damrosch, public art director for Portland's Regional Arts & Culture Council—discussed the goals of the art program. The belief that art "has the power to heal and give meaning to life and death" became the vision. The "Tree of Life" (ABOVE, RIGHT), designed by Frank Boyden and Brad Rude, appears above the fireplace in the main lobby. Birds fly out from its bronze branches and hover about the ceiling throughout the space. Boyden explains, "The 'Tree of Life' is a metaphor for this hospital. It harbors the many birds that rest on its branches. The birds leave and fly away from this tree, toward the hospital doors to outside life." THIS PAGE, BOTTOM: Interior elevation of perimeter wall and built-in window seats in main lobby. FOLLOWING PAGE: The interior of the main lobby is flooded with natural light. Patients and their families can relax or visit with friends in this airy, residential-scaled space.

# Level 7

**Lab, Outpatient Clinic, Pharmacy, Radiology, Rehabilitation**

THIS PAGE: Level 7 houses a variety of outpatient clinics, a pharmacy, labs, and diagnostic radiology and rehabilitation clinics. To maximize efficiency, the clinics were located one elevator stop above the main lobby. FOLLOWING PAGE: The waiting room located along the curved exterior wall serves the outpatient clinic with comfortable seating, play sculptures, and a direct connection to the outdoors. The art committee saw these spaces as opportunities to include interactive artworks, such as the alligator, designed by artist Rosalie Sherman.

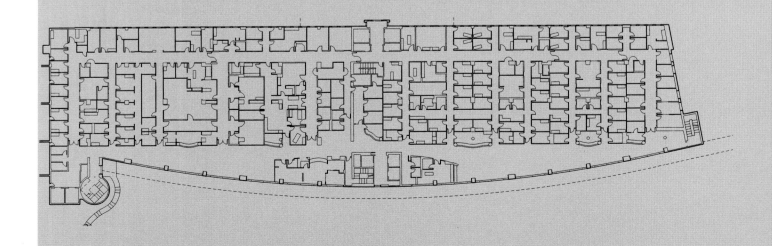

CDRC/Rehabilitation

PREVIOUS PAGE, ABOVE, LEFT AND RIGHT: Reception desks were carefully designed for both adults and children. Attention to the functional needs of patients and Doernbecher staff was a critical focus in the overall design. PREVIOUS PAGE, BELOW: Casework "castles" hold televisions, games, and aquariums in the waiting room activity areas for young patients and their siblings. These built-in shapes divide the large space into smaller living rooms, with waiting areas for both children and adults. THIS PAGE, RIGHT: Artist Rosalie Sherman designed the interactive alligator and turtle sculptures in the waiting areas. "I wanted to give the kids a chance to examine and become comfortable around a reptile...a chance to climb on a giant turtle's back...a chance to think of a great adventure instead of illness," she says. THIS PAGE, BELOW, LEFT: Artists Fernanda D'Agostino, Valerie Otani, and Elizabeth Stanek designed inquisitive peephole worlds. According to D'Agostino, "We wanted children to imagine windows they could slip through to a smaller, more secret world. In those worlds, a lunch box could be a house, and a shelf of books could contain the whole earth. A tablecloth could become a tent or the pasture for a flock of sheep." THIS PAGE, BELOW, RIGHT: Level 7 waiting area: partial furniture plan (TOP), interior elevations of built-in window seat along perimeter wall (CENTER), and reception desk (BOTTOM).

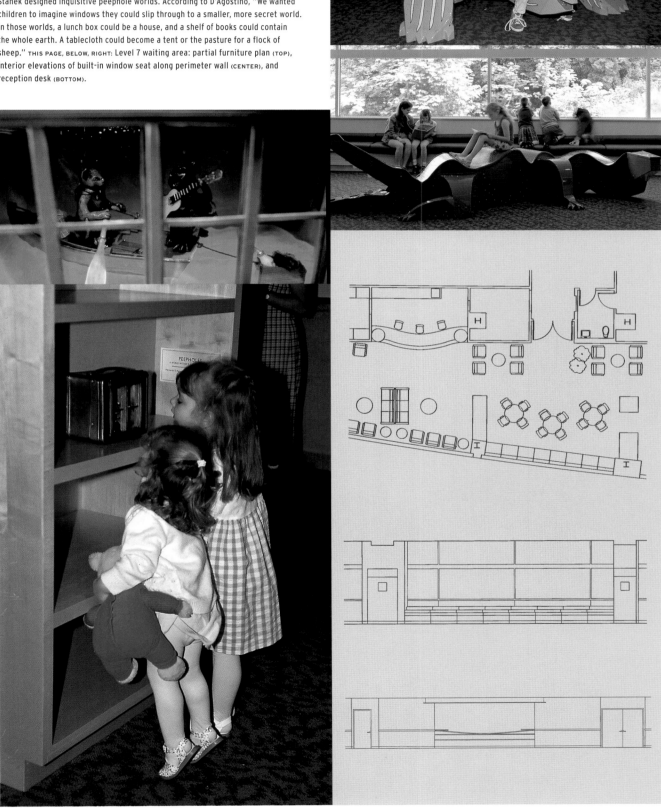

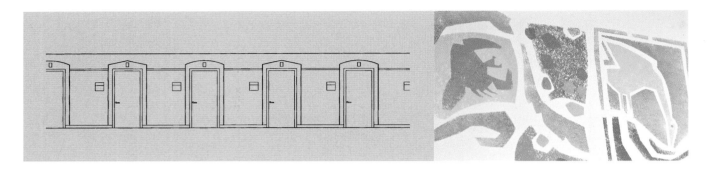

THIS PAGE, ABOVE, LEFT: Interior elevation of typical examination room corridor on Level 7. THIS PAGE, ABOVE, RIGHT: Brightly colored stenciling—designed by artists John Early and Laura Bender—borders the walls of the examination rooms, adding a humanistic touch. The natural themes of the stencils are scattered throughout the hospital. Each pattern is unique to its floor and complements the materials and finishes used on that level. THIS PAGE, BELOW: Distinctions between clinics are emphasized by the subtle use of colors, which serve as way-finding devices. For example, the same colors continue onto the floors of the examination and treatment rooms and around the doors, creating a visual continuity that directs patients to the appropriate destination. Custom-designed chart racks outside each examination room door are both functional and reflective of the "Animal World" theme on Level 7. FOLLOWING PAGE: The architects designed windowsill heights as low as possible to ensure that even the smallest child could enjoy views to the scenery outside. Metal wall sconces, designed by artists Suzanne Lee and Valerie Otani, cast colored light across the elevator lobby.

# Level 8

**Pediatric Intensive Care Unit, Surgery**

THIS PAGE: Level 8 houses the most critical care functions, including a 16-bed Pediatric Intensive Care Unit (PICU), day surgery, operating suites, cardiac diagnostic areas, recovery rooms, and family waiting areas. This is the first of two levels with direct access to OHSU Hospital, allowing children to be easily transported from the adjacent emergency department or heliport to Doernbecher's surgery area or PICU. FOLLOWING PAGE: Artist Margot Voorhies Thompson designed the ceramic frit pattern applied to the windows of the curving circulation spine. "I loved seeing how all the works came together in the end—the unexpected connections that were discovered after the fact. That is one of the great benefits of working in an environment of such enormous scale and purpose," she recalls. The images in the frit evolved from large-scale paintings commissioned for the public areas on Level 8.

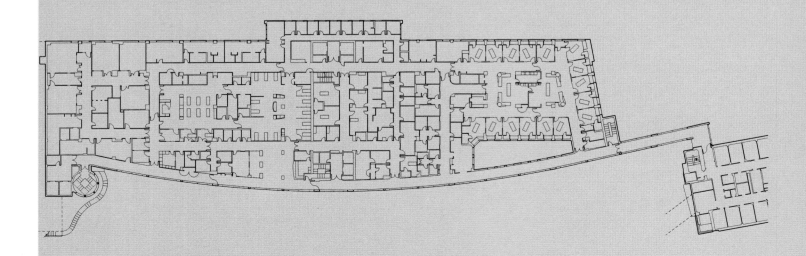

Surgery
Diagnostics
Pediatric ICU

Elevators

EXIT

PREVIOUS PAGE, ABOVE AND BELOW: Because of the critical nature of care on Level 8, there was a need for subtle variations in the family waiting areas. The waiting room is divided into three sections—an open seating area (ABOVE), a partially enclosed playroom (BELOW), and a fully-enclosed quiet waiting room. THIS PAGE, LEFT: Poet Kim Stafford dreamed of a small forest inside a building when he was a child. "At Doernbecher, I saw that dream again and wanted to put a poem there, [to be] with children and families." His words reflect the hospital's focus on connections to nature and family-centered care.

### NAKNUWISHA

"young friend
be part of something old—
be home here in the great world
where rain wants to give you drink
where forest wants to be your house
where frogs say your name and your name
where wee birds carry your wishes far
and the sun reaches for your hand—
be home here
be healed
be well
be with us all
young friend"

THIS PAGE, BELOW: Complementing the "Flora and Fauna" theme of Level 8, artist Margot Voorhies Thompson created a mural representing the four seasons. "I considered my work a success when I saw a young child drool on my painting ['Summer']; he had reached for the moth," she recalls.

THIS PAGE (CLOCKWISE): Plan of PICU nurse station; exterior windows in the operating rooms—a detail uncommon for this type of space—were a special request by the physicians, who often spend long hours performing complex surgeries; adjoining PICU suite doors also provide critical accessibility and visual connections between rooms, allowing nurses and physicians in adjacent areas to observe all patients in the unit; partial plan of floor pattern in PICU patient rooms; flexible Stage 1 and Stage 2 recovery beds accommodate changing inpatient and outpatient needs; the nurse stations were designed to provide clear visual connections into the patient rooms— an important consideration given the critical nature of care on this level. FOLLOWING PAGE, ABOVE: The nurse stations within the PICU feature soft curves and lowered desk heights, which help put parents at ease and give them a greater feeling of accessibility to Doernbecher staff. An uplifting color scheme was also used to alleviate the stress of this environment. FOLLOWING PAGE, BELOW: A fully enclosed waiting area provides an inviting, private space for family members visiting or waiting for PICU patients. A small garden offers visual relief for this stressful area of the hospital.

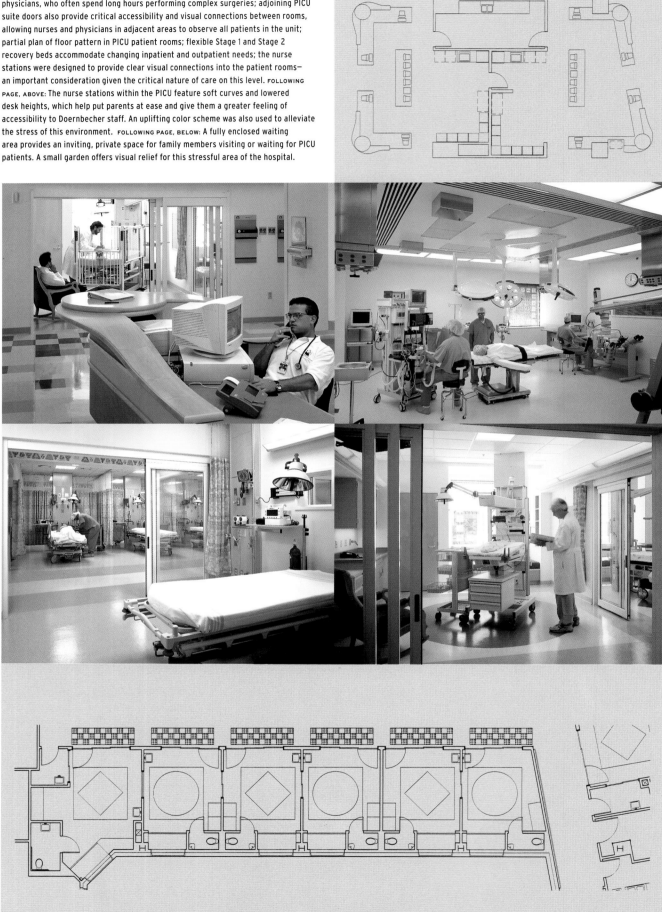

# Level 9

## Inpatient Nursing Units

THIS PAGE: Level 9 houses two 24-bed, inpatient nursing units, one for adolescents and the other for young children. A public connection to OHSU Hospital is provided at this level, with a direct link to that facility's main lobby. This floor also offers access to three different building courtyards: a child play space, a space reserved for staff, and one for patient families. FOLLOWING PAGE: The inpatient units reflect a residential concept; each room was designed as an individual "home." Every patient room is private, with a bathroom and bed for parents who want to stay with their child overnight. Interior windows framed in wood define the individuality of each room. Exterior windows offer views to the outdoors and provide a connection to nature.

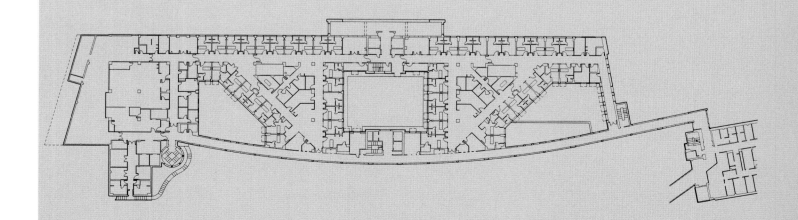

9 NORTH
ROOMS 25-48

PREVIOUS PAGE, ABOVE AND BELOW: The inpatient units reflect a "neighborhood" concept, with nurse stations located at each "intersection" and patient corridors serving as individual "streets." Every patient room is further identified by its own address board and a vinyl tile "doormat" outside its front door. On a broader scale, the triangular configuration effectively connects the various parts of the neighborhood, bringing together patients, family members, physicians, and staff. THIS PAGE, TOP: Interior elevation of typical inpatient corridor. THIS PAGE, MIDDLE, LEFT: Personal artwork or family photographs displayed on the address board at the entrance of every room reminds staff and visitors of each patient's individuality. A custom-designed chart rack for physicians and staff is part of the overall wall unit/address board. THIS PAGE, CENTER: This signage icon on Level 9 is a representation of the "Earth and Sky" theme. THIS PAGE, BOTTOM, LEFT: Partial plan of Level 9 entrance to patient room corridor. THIS PAGE, MIDDLE, RIGHT AND BOTTOM, RIGHT: Colorful, handmade tiles by artist Dana Lynn Louis decorate the walls of the private bathrooms in each patient room.

THIS PAGE, BELOW: ZGF redirected money in the architectural budget and engaged artist Margot Voorhies Thompson to design animated frit patterns for the perimeter of windowpanes in patient rooms and corridors on all floors. FOLLOWING PAGE, ABOVE AND BELOW: Each of the three interior courtyards is expressed in a slightly different manner, but the façades are all finished in warm stucco colors; fabric awnings shade the windows. The north courtyard is painted a soft yellow and designated for staff use.

PREVIOUS PAGE: The southern green courtyard is a designated quiet space where patients and their families can relax and reflect in a tranquil setting. THIS PAGE: The central rose-colored play courtyard has a gazebo (ABOVE AND BELOW, RIGHT), a fountain, and play equipment, all designed by artist Wayne Chabre, for use by patients and their visitors. "The [gazebo] creates a kind of dream environment, which celebrates escapism and the revival tent spirit. Birds are used as symbols of freedom, magic, and wisdom. At the apex of the roof is the bronze 'Guard Pigeon', braving the elements and representing a guardian spirit," explains the artist.

# Level 10

## Kenneth W. Ford Cancer Center, Inpatient Nursing Units, Meditation Room

THIS PAGE: Included on Level 10 is the Kenneth W. Ford Cancer Center, with a 16-bed inpatient unit and oncology clinic. The south end of the floor contains administrative offices, which can be converted to a nursing unit in the future.

FOLLOWING PAGE: A meditation room, created by artists Jim Hirschfeld and Sonya Ishii, is located on Level 10. Says Hirschfeld, "Inspiration for our meditation room sprang from the belief that silence and emptiness of space have the capacity to stimulate our imagination and focus our attention inward. The room's geometry and light create a luminous environment that warmly invites the visitor to spend time in contemplation."

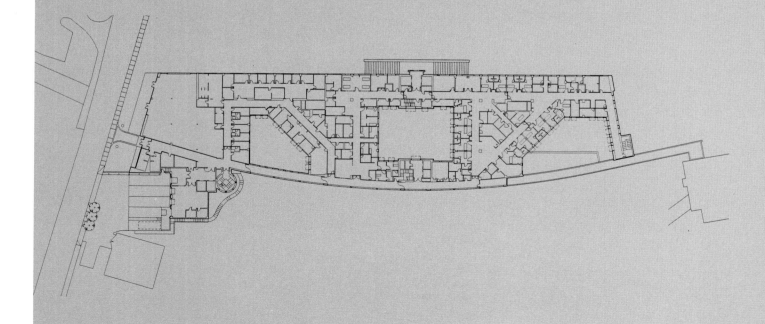

PREVIOUS PAGE, ABOVE, LEFT: The infusion rooms include beds and infusion chairs where patients can receive their treatment and rest. Play areas and views to the outdoors provide distractions for the patients, many of whom spend several hours in the unit under observation. PREVIOUS PAGE, ABOVE, RIGHT AND BELOW: In the waiting areas, furnishings in a variety of scales accommodate children and adolescents, as well as their families and visitors. Enclosed playrooms include aquariums, quiet reading spaces, and activity tables. THIS PAGE, ABOVE AND BELOW: A key goal of the art program was to carefully place works of art that would help soothe and distract patients during stressful situations. For example, illuminated shadow boxes by artists Valerie Otani and Suzanne Lee are incorporated into the ceilings of the patient elevator lobbies to help alleviate the anxiety of patients looking up from their gurneys. The artists also created colorful, stainless steel and glass relief panels on either side of the elevator doors on Levels 7 and 10.

# Level 11

Joseph Vey Conference Center

THIS PAGE: Level 11 is a partial
floor at the south end of the building.
FOLLOWING PAGE: The Joseph Vey
Conference Center provides a
150-seat auditorium and meeting facility
used for seminars, staff meetings,
and public events.

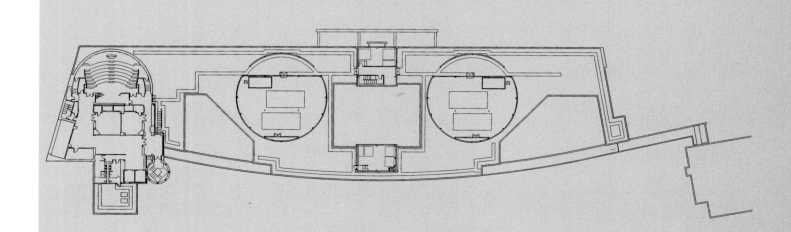

THIS PAGE, BELOW, LEFT AND RIGHT: Lounge and seating areas for staff and visitors also serve as breakout space where they can continue discussions initiated during seminars and conferences. A window wall provides visual and physical access to the outdoor terrace. THIS PAGE, CENTER, LEFT AND RIGHT: A flexible conference room that can be divided and configured in various ways is provided on level 11. THIS PAGE, BOTTOM, LEFT AND RIGHT: The Joseph Vey Conference Center helps fulfill the teaching and research mission of the hospital. The auditorium is designed around the concept of a "scientific conversation" between presenter and audience. Four camera positions provide video conferencing and interactive presentation capabilities. FOLLOWING PAGE: An outdoor terrace extends the architectural metaphor of an ocean liner.

# Acknowledgments

There is probably no building type more dependent on a diverse set of talents than a hospital that deals with the care and cure of diseases specific to children. In acknowledging the contributors to Doernbecher Children's Hospital, it is important to note that the functional and qualitative requirements were more interwoven than in any of our work in recent memory, and therein lies its success. Therefore, medical, nursing, and administrative staff can take as much pride in the physical result as the design team.

Although the entire group of contributors includes far too many staff and family members to list here, we would like to acknowledge a few individuals without whose commitment this program would not have approached its full potential.

Dr. Peter Kohler, the president of the Oregon Health Sciences University, recognized the need to expand the Doernbecher program for care and research. In recruiting Dr. Ron Rosenfeld as physician-in-chief, he found an individual of unusual talent and vision to lead this effort. Susanne Banz, the hospital administrator, worked with the architects and medical staff from the outset to assure that the building design fulfilled its program needs in the smallest detail. Our colleagues from Anshen + Allen, led by Derek Parker, worked with us on the medical planning and shared their experiences from previous pediatrics hospitals.

It is our wish that this monograph will contribute to the culture of sharing that is fundamental to medical research and healthcare, and, in some small way, that the act of documenting these experiences will make a difference beyond the Pacific Northwest.

—Bob Frasca

# Credits

## Doernbecher Children's Hospital, Portland, Oregon

Special thanks to all the Doernbecher staff and families who contributed to the design process

OWNER: Oregon Health Sciences University
PROJECT EXECUTIVE COMMITTEE: Dr. Peter Kohler, President; James Walker, Executive Vice President; Dr. Timothy Goldfarb, Director of Healthcare Systems; Gordon Ranta, Former Director of Facilities Design & Construction; Ric Nichols, Former Associate Hospital Director; Roy Vinyard, Former Chief Administrative Officer; Dr. Ron Rosenfeld, Chairman and Physician-in-Chief; Susanne Banz, Administrator, Doernbecher Children's Hospital; J.S. May, Former Director, Doernbecher Children's Hospital Foundation; Marvin Harrison, M.D., Pediatric Surgeon
ARCHITECT-OF-RECORD, DESIGN ARCHITECT AND INTERIOR DESIGNER: Zimmer Gunsul Frasca Partnership: Robert Packard, Associate AIA, Partner-in-Charge; Robert Frasca, FAIA, Design Partner; Bill Hutchinson, AIA, Project Manager; Allyn Stellmacher, AIA, Senior Designer; Jan Willemse, Senior Project Architect; Sharron van der Meulen, Senior Interior Designer; Terri Johnson, Associate IIDA, Senior Interior Designer
ZGF PROJECT TEAM: Larry Bruton, FAIA; Karl Sonnenberg, AIA; Jack Cornwall, AIA; Brooks Gunsul, FAIA; Eugene Sandoval; Charles Kelley, Jr., AIA; Robert Furusho; Robert Snyder, AIA; Ron Gronowski, AIA; Kathy Berg, AIA; Susan Kerns, IIDA; Carl Freeze, AIA; Heather Lindeen, Associate IIDA; Brian Stevens; Carolyn Cook
ASSOCIATE ARCHITECT, RESPONSIBLE FOR PROGRAMMING AND MEDICAL PLANNING: Anshen + Allen: Derek Parker, FAIA, RIBA; Felicia Borkovi, AIA; Annie Coull, AIA; Gary Marshall, AIA; Craig McInroy, AIA; Ian Lawlor, AIA; Gary Lukaszewski
GENERAL CONTRACTOR: Hoffman Construction Company: Don Smith, Project Executive; Bill Forsythe, Project Manager; Carl Reed, Project Superintendent; Richard Sells, Field Superintendent; Lou Parker, Senior Project Engineer; Brian Crosby, Project Engineer; Jeff Dawson, Project Engineer; Charlotte Salchenberg, Field Office Manager

ENGINEERS:
Structural/Civil Engineer: KPFF Consulting Engineers
ELECTRICAL ENGINEER/TELECOMMUNICATIONS: James D. Graham & Associates
MECHANICAL ENGINEER: Manfull-Curtis, Inc.
GEOTECHNICAL ENGINEER: Geo Engineers, Inc.

OTHER SPECIAL CONSULTANTS:
SIGNAGE: Anderson Krygier, Inc.
LANDSCAPE ARCHITECT: Walker & Macy
HEALTHCARE CONSULTANT/SPACE PROGRAM: M. Bostin Associates, Inc. (owner's consultant)
EQUIPMENT PLANNERS: Medical Equipment Planning
ACOUSTICAL CONSULTANT: Altermatt Associates
LIGHTING DESIGNER: Candela
FOOD SERVICE: Cini-Little International, Inc.
TRANSPORTATION/TRAFFIC/PARKING: Carl Buttke, Inc.
CONVEYING SYSTEMS: Lerch Bates & Associates
SURVEYING: Hickman Williams
DOERNBECHER ART COMMITTEE: Jane Beebe, Chairperson; Eloise Damrosch, Public Art Director, Regional Arts & Culture Council, Program Manager; Jan Crider; Mary Ann Lockwood; Robert Frasca; Joan Gray; Bill Hutchinson; J.S. May; Gordon Ranta; Deanne Rubinstein; Diana Schmitt; Allyn Stellmacher; Ralph Tuomi; Janet Webster; Louise Weiss; Barbara Stafford Wilson
ARTISTS: Laura Bender; Frank Boyden; Wayne Chabre; Fernanda D'Agostino; John Early; Jim Hirschfield; Sonya Ishii; Suzanne Lee; Dana Lynn Louis; Valerie Otani; Brad Rude; Rosalie Sherman; Kim Stafford; Elizabeth Stanek; Margot Voorhies Thompson
PHOTOGRAPHERS: Timothy Hursley; Pete Eckert/Eckert & Eckert; Bergman Photographic Services